ORGANIZATION

OF

A NEW INDIAN TERRITORY,

EAST OF THE MISSOURI RIVER.

ARGUMENTS AND REASONS SUBMITTED TO THE HONORABLE THE MEMBERS OF THE SENATE AND HOUSE OF REPRESENTATIVES OF THE 31st CONGRESS OF THE UNITED STATES:

BY

THE INDIAN CHIEF KAH-GE-GA-GAH-BOUH,

OR

GEO. COPWAY.

NEW YORK:

S. W. BENEDICT, No. 16 SPRUCE STREET.

1850.

MR. COPWAY'S PLAN.

To the Honorable the Senate and House of Representatives of the Thirty-first Congress of the United States:

GENTLEMEN:—The history of a nation is always interesting. The more obscure the means of tracing it, the more of interest attaches to it, as it slowly discloses itself to the eye of research.

The past of American history is to every meditative man full of silent instruction. The struggle between the two races, the European and the American, has been in steady progress since their first intercourse with each other. The pale-face has bequeathed his history's bloody page to his children after him. The Indians, on the other hand, have related the story of their wrongs to their children in the lodge, and have invariably taught them to look upon a pale-face as a hard brother.

The account of their hatred to each other in years long past, is, no doubt, without foundation. Its relation has, however, had the evil tendency of embittering one against the other, has kept them at variance, and prevented them from learning of each other those noble qualities which *all* will acknowledge each possessed.

What a change! The progress of aggression has gone on with its resistless force westward with emigration, from the time the first colony was planted on the Atlantic's shores. Wave after wave has rolled on, till now there appears no limit to the sea of population. The North resounds with the woodman's axe; the South opens its valleys to make room for the millions that are swarming from the Old World to the New.

The rivers that once wound their silent and undisturbed

course beneath the shades of the forest, are made to leave their natural ways, and, bending to the arbitrary will of man, follow the path he marks out for them. Man labors, and gazes in astonishment at the mighty work his hands perform—he gazes at the complicated machinery he has set in motion. The Indian is out of sight—he sends no horror to the pale-face by his shrill war-whoop, nor pity by the wail of his death-song.

Steam thunders along over hills and vales that once were peaceful—on, on, to the mighty West.

The groans of the Indian are occasionally heard by the intoxicated and avaricious throng in the way of complaint; he has waited for justice, while those who have wronged him, like the wild horses of his prairie, neigh over his misfortunes.

The eagle of liberty stretches her wings north and south. The tide of emigration will soon reach the base of the Rocky Mountains and rise to the summit. Enterprise follows in its train; yet when blessings are lavishly bestowed on the pale-faces, as the consequence of attainments in knowledge, the red-man has been denied the least of those which the American government guarantees to its humblest subject.

These thoughts have arisen in my mind previous to calling the attention of the Members of this Congress to a plan for the effectual consolidation of the western tribes, with a view to their temporal and spiritual improvement.

Before stating the plan, which I have already laid before the American people, as the only means which can be used to save the Indians from extinction, I shall, in as brief a manner as possible, give a few reasons why they have not materially improved, and why their numbers have been greatly lessening.

1. *Why has not the Indian improved when coming in contact with civilization?* To give a statement of all the disadvantages he has had to encounter would not be in accordance with my present object; I will mention a few. In their intercourse with the frontier settlers they meet the worst classes of pale-faces. They soon adopt their foolish ways and their vices, and their minds being thus poisoned and pre-occupied, the morality and education which the better classes would teach them are forestalled. This will not be wondered at

when it is generally known that the frontier settlements are made up of wild, adventurous spirits, willing to raise themselves by the downfall of the Indian race. These are traders, spirit-sellers, horse-thieves, counterfeiters, and scape-gallowses, who neither fear God nor regard man. When the Indians come in contact with such men, as representatives of the American people, what else could be expected from them? They scarcely believe that any good can come out of such a Nazareth as they think the United States to be; and all are aware that man is more prone to learn from others their vices than their virtues. It is not strange, that, seeing as he does the gross immorality of the white men whom he meets, and the struggle between the pale-face for wrong and the red-man for right, which begins when they first meet, and ends not until one dies, that he refuses to follow in the footsteps of the white man.

"What!" said an Indian to me once, in the North-west, when I was endeavoring to convince him of the necessity of schooling his children, "shall my children be taught to lie, steal, kill, and quarrel, as the white man does? No, no," he continued, shaking his head. Having never been in the midst of refined and civilized society, he knew not of its blessings. He judged from what he saw around him, and with such examples, he decided rightly.

There has been one class of adventurers who have moved westward, whose fathers were murdered by the Indians. These having an implacable hatred against the poor Indian, do all they can to enrage one race against the other, and if possible involve the two in war, that they may engage in their favorite work of depredation.

2. *Their love of adventurous life.* The suddenness with which a band of white men has ever intruded upon them, has prevented them from gradually acquiring the arts of civilized life; and leaving local employment, they have hunted for a living, and thus perpetuated that independent, roaming disposition, which was their early education. Their fathers having been Nimrods, in a literal sense, they followed in their steps. Not that I would have you suppose that there is no such thing as

teaching the American Indian the peaceful arts of agriculture, for he has already proved himself teachable.

3. *The perpetual agitation of mind which they experience in the annoyance they receive from mischievous men, and the fear of being removed westward by the American government.* None but an Indian can, perhaps, rightly judge of the deleterious influence which the repeated removals of the Indians has wrought, since they began in the days of Jefferson, in 1804, and have been continued by succeeding administrations, until the last. Here let me say to Members of Congress, Mature a pacific policy, for the mutual good of the red man and the white man. Let each love the other with the same spirit that animated the bosom of William Penn, and we shall yet have many sunny days—days when the white man and the red man shall join hands, and together, as brothers, go up yet higher on the mount of noble greatness. Fear has prevented the Indian from making any very great advancement in agricultural science. Having seen the removal of many tribes, he is conscious of the fact, that the government may, and doubtless will, want more land, and they be obliged to sell at whatever price government may see fit to give, and thus all improvements they may have made become valueless to them.

The missionaries, in many instances, have done nobly in subduing the wild and warring disposition of many of the Indians, but these lessons have all been lost by the removal of the Indian west. And if he say aught, he is represented by the agent in an antagonistic attitude toward his government, and the Indians become the sufferers.

4. *The want of schools of the character that are required for the education of the Indians.* You will, no doubt, tell me that the Indians have been taught the advantages of education—that some have even attended, not only the common school, but schools of a higher order and colleges, and have returned again to the forest, have put on the blanket and roamed the woods. This has not always been the case. I might name a great many, who, to my knowledge, have done well, and are doing well for themselves and for their people.

I have never heard of any inquiry having been made by

any society or government, as to what is the best mode of education for Indian youth. My opinion may differ from that of more aged and experienced men, yet after much observation and inquiry, I am convinced that the three most requisite things for an Indian youth to be taught, are a good mechanical trade, a sound code of morality, and a high-toned literature.

The reason of their returning back again, was the absence of a good moral training, and their not having learned any trade with which to be employed on their leaving the schools. Having no employment and no income, they found themselves in possession of all the qualities of a gentleman, without the requisite funds to support themselves.

Their training in moral culture had not been attended to, because some of those men who had been their instructors knew Christianity by theory only, not by a practical knowledge of the pleasing and persuasive influence of the Bible.

The Indian ought not to be allowed to stand still in the way of improvement; for if he does not advance, he will surely recede, and lose the knowledge he may already have attained. Let him taste the pleasures of education, and he will, if proper care be taken at the commencement, drink deep of the living spring.

5. *The great quantity of land which they have reserved to themselves for the purpose of hunting.* This wide field, filled with a variety of game, perpetuates their natural propensities to live by the use of the bow or gun, instead of the hoe or plow; to roam the fields instead of having a local habitation. When they have land that they can call their own, and limited, so that the scarcity of game will oblige them to till the soil for a subsistence, then they will improve, and the sooner this state of affairs is brought about, the better.

Some of my Indian brethren may wonder that I should offer this as one of my reasons, and my white brethren may think that I would limit the Indian to rather narrow quarters. If any argument I now bring forward will not bear investigation, why, throw it out. I but write what in my humble judgment is an impartial view of the subject, and state plans which I think best adapted to advance the interests of all, and which should be adopted in order to elevate the condition of the Indians of America.

6. *The mode generally adopted for the introduction of Christianity among the Indians.* This mode has not, I think, been one that would induce them to speedily relinquish their habits of life. I am aware that I here tread on delicate ground. There is zeal enough among the missionaries who labor among them to move the world, if there were any *system* of operation. There is piety enough to enkindle and fan to a blaze the fine devotional feelings of the Indians, if there were one uniform course taken by all those who go to teach them.

The *doctrines* which have been preached in this civilized country may be necessary for the purpose of stimulating various denominations to zealous labor, but in our country they have had a tendency to retard the progress of the gospel. The strenuous efforts that have been made to introduce doctrinal views, and forms of worship, have perplexed and prejudiced the mind of the Indian against Christianity.

It is true that every man who has been among the Indians as a missionary to them has not been as judicious as he should have been. The idea that *anything* will do for the Indian, has also been a mistaken one.

We want men of *liberal education* as well as of devoted piety. It is not requisite that a missionary carry with him the discipline of churches, but it *is* requisite that he carry with him consistency, in order to meet with success among the Indian tribes.

When they preach love to God and to all men, and act otherwise toward ministers of differing denominations, it creates doubts in the mind of the watchful Indian as to the truth of the word he hears. Let the men advocating the sacred cause of God go on together, let them labor side by side for the good of the Indian, and he will soon see that they intend his good. The Indian is not willfully blind to his own interests.

I have tried to convince the different missionaries that it is better to teach the Indians in English, rather than in their own language, as some have done and are now doing. A great amount of *time* and *money* have been expended in the translation of the Bible into various languages, and afterward the Indian has been taught to read; when he might have been taught English in much less amount of time and with less expenditure of money. Besides this, the few books that have been translated into our language are the *only books* which they *can* read, and in this are perpetuated his views, ideas and feelings; whereas, had he been taught English, he would have been introduced into a wide field of literature; for so *very* limited would be the literature of his own language, that he could have no scope for his powers; consequently, the sooner he learned the almost universal English and forgot the Indian, the better. If the same policy is pursued that has been, the whole of the world's history must be translated into Indian, and the Indian be taught to read it before he can know the story of the past.

There are other reasons that might be given, why the condition of the Indian has not improved, did space allow. I proceed to give the reasons for the gradual diminution of their numbers since their first intercourse with the whites, three hundred and fifty-six years ago.

1. *Diseases introduced by Europeans.* They had no knowledge of the *small-pox,* measles, and *other* epidemics of civilization's growth. The small-pox destroyed the Mandans, a tribe once occupying the shores of the upper waters of the Missouri, in '37 and '38. Entire families perished. American history relates many a distressing fact in relation to that ill-fated tribe. Foreign disease has preyed on the vitals of the Indian, and he knew not what remedies to use to arrest its progress, however skillful he might have been in curing the infirmities which were found with him. He knew no cure for the new diseases that ravaged among them.

2. *Wars among themselves since the introduction of fire-arms among them.* The weapons they used, previous to their meeting the whites, were not as destructive as the rifle. With the gun they have been as expert as they were with

the bow and arrow. Champlain, in the year 1609, supplied the Algonquin tribes of the north with weapons of war for them to subdue the Six Nations, and the Dutch supplied the Six Nations in the now State of New York. The Spaniards of the South, and others, might be cited. They received these weapons of war from civilized nations, guaranteeing to them the free use of them.

3. *The wars among the white people of this country.* During these wars the Indian has been called to show his fearless nature ; and for obeying, and showing himself true to the code of a warrior, as he understood it, he has been called a *savage*, by the very men who needed his aid and received it. In the midst of these contests the Indians have been put in the front ranks, in the most dangerous positions, and have consequently been the greatest losers.

4. *The introduction of spirituous liquors.* This has been another, and perhaps greater than all other evils combined. The *fire-water* has done a most disastrous work, and the glad shout of the Indian boy has been hushed as he bended over the remains of his father, whose premature death has been brought on by its use. The Indian has not sufficient moral fortitude to withstand its evil seductiveness. Disease, war, and famine have preyed upon individual life, but alcoholic drinks have cut off from the list of nations many whose records are inscribed on the face of the mountain.

Peace and happiness entwined around the firesides of the Indian once—union, harmony, and a common brotherhood cemented them to each other. But as soon as these vile drinks were introduced among them dissipation commenced, and the ruin and downfall of a noble race went on. Every year lessened its numbers. The trader found this to be one of the easiest means of securing him rich gains. Wave after wave of destruction invaded the wigwam of the Indian, while the angel of death hovered over his lodge-fires with its insatiable thirst for victims.

In mockery of his wrongs, the eye of the distant observer has looked on the destruction of the Indian, and when he saw him urged to desperate deeds, the white man would calmly say, "Ah, the Indian will be an Indian still."

You say he loves it so well that it is impossible to keep it from him. There was a time when the cool water from the mountain tops was all that allayed his thirst. He loved that, because the Great Spirit sent it to him.

Traders carry the fire-water into the western country by hundreds of barrels, and it has become a common saying among the Indians, "If you see a white man, you will see a jug of rum."

The tide of avaricious thirst for gold rolls on, and the trader resorts to those means to satisfy it, that bring upon the Indian poverty, misery, and death. One reason why the gospel has not been more readily received is, because the Indians have not been allowed to remain in a condition to hear and understand it.

The fears I entertain that the Indians will never have a permanent hold upon any part of their lands are from the following reasons.

1. *Their position before the press of emigration.* Their rights will be trampled upon by new settlers, and this, with other annoyances they may receive, will unsettle their minds, and consequently they will remove step by step to escape such annoyance.

The present belief of the Indians is, that they will never again be removed, and that the land they now have is to be their own forever. But American enterprise will require railroads to be built, canals to be opened, military roads to be laid out through that western country, and this land will be demanded. The Indians will soon see that their permanency will be destroyed, and they will cease to improve the soil; since such labor would not be for their own benefit, but for the benefit of the white men who are crowding upon them.

The superior quality of the land for agricultural purposes, will also be an inducement for the emigrant to use all possible endeavors to obtain it.

2. *The quantity of the land* always has and always will retard the progress of their civilization. The game on those

lands being abundant, will induce them to neglect the improvement of the soil, which otherwise they would attend to. What do we want land for, when the quantity we possess is a preventive to our improving any particular portion of it?

3. *Necessity will oblige them to sell.* They have ever reasoned thus: Our fathers sold their lands to the government and lived on the proceeds of the sale, and soon the government will want to buy this land, and our children will live on their annuities as we now do on ours; so they will fare as well as we have. In this way they become improvident.

4. *The scarcity of food when the game has gone.* This will produce trouble between the Indians and the white people of the West. However desirous the government may be to maintain peace with the Indians, it will itself occasion the trouble it so much fears.

The game is being killed more and more every year. It is computed by recent travelers, that one hundred thousand buffaloes are killed by trappers for their tongues and hides, which are sold to traders up the Missouri. Game of all kinds is fast disappearing from this side of the mountains. When, by force of circumstance, the Indian is forced to live on the cattle of the frontier settlers, as soon as the first bullock is killed, the cry will be heard, "The Indians are coming! To arms! to arms!" and the soldiery of the United States must be sent to destroy them. The boom of a thousand cannon, the rattle of the drum, and the trumpet's blast, will be heard all over the western prairies; the fearful knell that tells of the downfall of a once noble race.

Desperation will drive the Indian to die at the cannon's mouth, rather than "*remove*" beyond the Rocky Mountains.

Should this time come, (God grant it never may,) the paleface must not be surprised should he hear the battle cry resound from peak to peak, and see them descending upon the frontiers, to avenge their wrongs and regain their once happy possessions.

5. *Their isolated condition.* This will be perpetuated as long as the American government addresses them as distinct tribes. It should, instead of this, treat them as one nation.

Not till they amalgamate, will they lose the hostile feelings they now have for each other.

Having, in as few words as possible, given the causes which, in my opinion, have prevented them from improving, have decreased their numbers, and the foundation of my fears that they are yet in a critical situation, I will state the plan I have drawn up, and which I have been laying before the American people during the past year. I have had the honor of addressing legislative bodies from South Carolina to Massachusetts, as also the people of various cities and towns.

My object is to induce the general government to locate the Indians in a collective body, where, after they are secured in their lands, they may make such improvements as shall serve to attach them to their homes.

This will be more applicable to the Indians of the North-west than to those of the Southwest; *for I would not be understood as thinking or legislating for the civilized portion, who are by far the most enlightened of the American Indians.*

The questions naturally arise, When and how can this be accomplished? Is it practicable?

I feel that I am inadequate to perform the task of showing plainly the *place* where they ought to be settled, as well as the *manner* in which it is to be brought about. Different individuals will have different opinions on these points.

The location which I have chosen for their home, is the unsettled land, known as the North-west Territory, between the territories of Nebraska and Minnesota, on the eastern banks of the Missouri river. The great Sioux river being the eastern boundary, from its head waters draw a line westward until it meets the Missouri river; thence down the Missouri to the place of beginning. This would form an Indian territory large enough for all the scattered tribes of Michigan Wisconsin, Iowa, &c.

The reasons why I have named this as the most suitable location for them are the following:

I would not be understood as dictating as to the country, where they are to form a nucleus of settlements. It is the idea with some that in the upper waters of the Mississippi river, would likely be the place. But my own ideas differ much from this. Because the upper waters of the Mississippi are going to be the greatest source of lumber trade, and the races coming in contact with one another must cause trouble along the river.

They will go away from the course of emigration which goes up the Missouri and thence westward. They would be two hundred and fifty miles north of this trail. The climate is best for them. Either north or south would not do. In the first, they would suffer from cold; in the last, from sickness.

The distance of this territory westward would cause their removal to be gradual, and by the time the whites should reach there, the Indians would be so far improved as to be enabled to live as neighbors, and could compete with the whites in point of intelligence, and mechanical and agricultural skill.

The last, but not the least question which arises, is this,

Is IT PRACTICABLE? I think it is.

1. Their interests being in the hands of the United States government, the government would have an influence for good in reference to their annuities. By an annual distribution of these, they would become attached to the place of concentration.

2. All the treaties, having for their end the removal of the Indians, may be made with an understanding, that they are never to be moved again, should they go. This would be one of the greatest inducements that could be presented to them, and they would soon go. They are not stubborn beings. Convince them it is for their good, and you will speedily attain your object.

3. The Indians are a social race. They would rather live in large bodies than in small ones, particularly when they are partially civilized. The oftener they see one another, the more rapidly would their jealousies cease to exist. Their children, growing up together, would acquire a mutual attachment and a mutual regard for each other's welfare.

4 The language of the northwest tribes is peculiarly

adapted for such a state of society; they would soon understand each other, the Ojibwa language being the great family language of all the Algonquin tribes west. This is one of the best appeals I made to them when I visited them. Tradition says we were all one people once, and now to be re-united will be a great social blessing. Wars must then cease.

5. By giving encouragement to those who would go there to settle, there would be no difficulty in getting them there, for the educated portion of them would be the first to go and lay the foundation for a settlement. And such are those whom I would have go, for they do so from good motives.

6. Should they not be induced to go in collective bodies? A proclamation from the President of the United States, calling upon all the northwest tribes to till the ground, as they must soon have recourse to farming for a living, would induce them individually to go without the chiefs, and they would, as soon as they entered the new territory, frame laws founded on republicanism. The hereditary chiefship must cease to exist, before they can make any rapid advancement; for when you allow the meritorious only to rule, there will be found a great many who will study hard to improve in general information, and fit themselves for statesmen and divines.

Having stated the reasons why I deem my scheme practicable, I will, in conclusion, allude to the advantages that would accrue, not only to the United States, but to the Indians.

To the American Government.

1. This system would simplify the Indian department.

2. They would not have so much perplexity in adjusting difficulties.

3. The outlay in Indian agencies would be lessened.

4. Establish a court of justice in the Indian territory, and no trouble would be had with them, as the difficulties would be legally settled. For sometimes it has been the hasty means used to suppress the encroachments of the Indian on the white man which have caused the disgraceful wars which this country has seen. Such would be obviated.

5. The expense of fortifying the western country from the encroachments of the Indians would be dispensed with, and even now they are not actually required. But if the government *must* build forts, and establish military posts, let there be one, in the center of the new Indian territory, to give efficiency to the laws of the Indian government, to protect the peace and persons in that country.

Go in the spirit of the illustrious William Penn, that noble personification of Christianity, and you will have no trouble with the Indians this side of the Rocky Mountains.

6. The outlay for transporting the Indians would cease to be a burden. I believe the Indians would now go of their own accord, did they know that the land could be thus occupied by them.

7. The buying of the land from the Indians over and over would not then have to be done.

8. The peaceful and friendly relations that must then exist would be one of the strongest bonds of union in time of peace, and cause them to be neutral in time of war.

9. Besides the above considerations, there are higher motives which ought to prompt the members of Congress,—motives arising in the consideration that you are only forwarding the great design of Heaven, to improve the races of this country. By intelligence enlarge the arena of human freedom, and your leading the Indian may be like the noble eagle's first flight with its young to the sun.

The advantages to the Indians.

1. By having *permanent* homes they would soon enjoy the fruit of their labor. Poverty would be unknown, plenty would reign, and cheerfulness aid them in their work.

2. Seminaries of learning would be permanently located; every stone you laid for the foundation of a school would tell. The repeated removals of the Indians have retarded the progress of moral and physical training among them, and caused many good men to become discouraged in their alms-giving for their improvement. It has not been so much the fault of the Indian as it has been the error of judgment in the distribution of these means.

3. The appropriation by the United States, for the education of the Indians, of $10,000, would then be a benefit to those for whom it is intended. Let the government endow a college in the central part of the Indian country, and it would have an influence for good to the end of time.

4. And besides this, what an amount would accumulate, were all the school funds which the Indians have even now, given by the government in its generosity for their annuities, and which now many Indian tribes know not what to do with, thus appropriated. Concentration of means and of effort on the part of the benevolently-disposed, must necessarily, in the process of time, do a great deal of good.

5. In treaties which are to be made, if a policy could be pursued in such a way as to get the annuities of the Indians to be paid in part toward the national education of the whole colony, much of what is needed in reference to means would be so augmented as to give whole districts of country the benefit of an enlightened education.

But say you, How will you reconcile the different denominations of Christians who may go there to teach?

Having no predilection to *division* and discord, I would not have one dollar of the money which the generosity of the government should give, go toward perpetuating discordant elements. No! I want to make the great family of the Indians ONE, should I live long enough—*one* in interest, *one* in feeling, *one* while they live, and *one* in a better world after death.

6. Emulation among themselves would spring up; and each would labor for the other's good, a spirit of rivalry would soon be seen were a premium to be given to those who should raise the largest amount of agricultural produce.

7. The result of all this would be a rapid increase of intelligence among the Indians, and steps would soon be taken to have a representation in Congress.

It is hoped that, without making any special plea for the red men, that sense of justice which dwells in the heart of every *true American* will lead the members of Congress to give the above reasons a passing consideration.

GENTLEMEN:—I herein place before you a Bill which I have drawn up by the request of the Members of the last Indian Committee of the House of Representatives, of last session, which might serve to suggest in the minds of your honorable body, the features of a Bill, and such other additions and alterations as the wisdom of Congress may devise.

A BILL TO PROVIDE FOR THE ORGANIZATION OF AN INDIAN TERRITORY EAST OF THE MISSOURI RIVER.

Be it enacted by the Senate and House of Representatives of the United States, in Congress assembled,

That all of that part of the territory of the United States, bounded on the *east* by the great Sioux river, from its junction with the Missouri up to its source; on the *north* by a line from the source of the great Sioux river, westward until it strikes the Missouri river, down the channel of said river as the *western* boundary, to the junction of Missouri river, or place of beginning; shall constitute a Territory to be called "The Kah-ge-ga* Indian Territory."

Section 2d. And be it further enacted, That the said territory shall be forever hereafter reserved for the use of the various tribes who may have a right to the same, and the faith of the United States is hereby pledged, that all that part of said territory which has been or may be granted to any of the Indian tribes, shall be, and the same is hereby secured to them and to their heirs and descendants forever; and the United States will cause a grant or patent to be made and executed for the same—and in case any two or more tribes, the grant to such tribes shall inure to the benefit of such united

* KAH-GE-GA, an Indian name of firm, or ever; which would mean "Ever-to-be Indian Territory."

tribes shall agree upon. Provided, That such lands shall revert to the general Confederation, if the Indians, for whose benefit such have been or may be made, should become extinct or should abandon them.

Section 3*d*. And be it further enacted, That each of the tribes residing within the said territory, may establish and maintain such government for the regulation of their own internal affairs, as to them may seem proper; not inconsistent with the Constitution of the United States, or the Laws thereof.

Section 4*th*. And be it further enacted, That until otherwise provided by the people of said territory, through the general Council, and with the approval of Congress, a government of the said territory shall be appointed by the President, with a resident Indian to be styled Lieutenant Governor, by and with the advice and consent of the Senate, who shall be, *ex-officio*, Superintendent of the Indian Affairs of said territory for the term of three years, and who shall take an oath of office, and shall receive as Governor and Superintendent an annual salary of three thousand five hundred dollars; and the salary of the Lieutenant Governor, to be annual, two thousand five hundred dollars, which shall be in full of all charges, allowances, and emoluments of whatever nature or kind. And the said Governor and Lieutenant Governor to reside at such place within said territory as may be selected by those occupying it, and shall execute such duties as may be enjoined by laws, or as may be directed by the Governor and Council, approved of by the President.

Section 5*th*. And be it further enacted, That a Secretary of the said territory shall be appointed by the President, by and with the advice and consent of the Senate, for the term of four years, who shall take an oath of office, and shall receive an annual compensation of fifteen hundred dollars, which shall be in full of all charges, allowances, and emoluments of whatever kind and nature; and it shall be the duty of the Secretary to reside at the place appointed for the residence of the Governor; he shall keep a record of all the official proceedings of the Governor and Lieutenant Governor of the said territory, and annually transmit copies of the same to the Houses of Congress; he shall discharge the duties of Governor of said territory, provided the Lieutenant Governor is away, who is to discharge the duties *ex-officio* during the absence of the Governor or vacation of the office, and shall fulfill all other duties as shall be enjoined by law.

Section 6th. And be it further enacted, That as soon as may be, after his appointment, the said Governor and Lieutenant Governor shall convene at some proper point, a sufficient number of the chiefs or other representatives of the various tribes, who may reside within the said territory, and shall submit to them for their assent, such of the provisions of this Act as require the co-operation of the authorities of the respective tribes, in order to carry the same into effect, and such assent, if given, shall be in writing and in duplicate; one of which duplicates shall be preserved in the office of said Governor. Provided, The articles of confederation shall not be binding upon any tribe unless assented to by the chiefs of such tribes, being previously authorized thereto, or unless they shall be ratified by such tribe. Provided also, That such confederation shall not take effect until the tribes assenting thereto shall, in the aggregate, number at least one-fourth of the whole amount, and thereafter other tribes in said territory may join said confederation and become members thereof.

Section 7th. And be it further enacted, That a general Council of the tribes giving their assent and forming the confederacy thus provided, shall be annually held at such time and place as may be fixed on by the Governor and Lieutenant Governor; the said Council shall consist of not less than one nor more than five delegates from any tribe, who shall be elected by the respective tribes or selected from the existing chiefs, in proportion to their numbers, which proportion shall be determined by the Governor; the Lieutenant Governor shall preside over the general Council, which shall have power to make all needful regulations respecting the intercourse among the several tribes, to preserve peace, to provide for their common safety, and generally to enact such laws as the welfare of the confederation shall demand, and as may be necessary to give effect to the purpose of this Act, not inconsistent with the Constitution of the United States; all the laws and regulations adopted by the said Council shall be submitted to the Governor for his consideration, and shall have no force unless approved by him; the Governor shall also have power to convene the said Council upon extraordinary occasions, and at all times to adjourn it; and the members of the Council shall, until otherwise provided, receive from the United States three dollars each, per day, during the attendance at the session thereof, and their reasonable expenses, to be settled by the Governor, in going to and returning therefrom. Provided, That nothing herein contained shall interfere with the right of the general government to regulate the trade and intercourse between the United States and the Indian tribes within said territory.

Section 8th. And be it further enacted, That all officers and persons in the service of the United States, and all persons employed under treaty stipulation, and all persons traveling in or through said territory, and not residents thereof, shall be under the protection of and subject to the laws of the United States, and that they be required to have the usual license to be issued by the agent or agents, to be appointed by the President of the United States; and if any such officer or person shall, within said territory, commit any offense against the laws of any tribe of this confederacy, he may be tried and punished under the laws of said tribe, subject however to the approval of the government, who may confirm or remit the said judgment, or remove such offender from the limits of said tribe. Provided, That when the penalty be death, the judgment shall be forthwith communicated to the President by the Governor, who shall suspend the execution thereof until the pleasure of the President be known; and whenever an Indian of one tribe, or any other person residing therein, except as above provided, shall commit a capital offense upon a member or resident of another tribe, he shall be apprehended, tried and punished in such manner as shall be previously provided by the general Council.

Section 9th. And be it further enacted, That in accordance with pledges heretofore given in treaty with some of the Indian tribes herein proposed to be erected into a Territorial Government, to promote their advancement, protect their interests, and bind them more closely to the government of the United States, it shall be competent for the said confederate tribes to elect in such manner as the general Council shall prescribe, a delegate or commissioner to the Congress of the United States, or government of the same, who shall have the same powers, privileges and compensation as is usual in delegates or commissioners from any territories to have.

Section 10th. And be it further enacted, That it shall be lawful for any of the tribes entering into the confederacy, or the general Council, to adopt as the laws of such tribes or confederacy, any or all of the prohibiting provisions of the laws of the United States regulating trade or intercourse with the Indians and Indian tribes, with such penalties as shall be approved by the Governor, and establish a tribunal for the trial of offenders against the same, and it shall be the duty of the Governor to use all necessary means to carry the same into effect.

Section 11*th.* And be it further enacted, That the government of the United States shall establish in the center of said territory a military post of sufficient force for the protection of the inhabitants thereof, as well as to secure the Indians from the lawless, and that the officers and persons in the service of the United States so employed, shall be exempt from the previous act of the license of travelers.

Section 12*th.* And be it further enacted, That nothing in this Act shall be construed as authorizing or directing the violation of any existing treaty between the United States and any of the Indian tribes; nor shall anything in this Act be construed as changing the relation now existing between the United States and any tribe within said territory, which shall not become a member of said confederacy.

The recommendations of the Presidents for these ten or fifteen years back, and the action of the various Indian commissioners on the subject, has induced me to take up the subject, with the idea of benefiting the general interest of the Indians, and accommodating alike the American government.

My observations in the West, during the past season in Wisconsin, Minnesota, Iowa, and the valley of the Missouri, induce me to be sanguine, that whatever arrangement Congress may make for the Indians, for their good, will be hailed with approbation by the North-western Settlers, the missionaries, traders, governors, and others alike interested in the Indians.

As I did not receive an official authority from the present

administration before I went to the North-west on a visit to all the Indian tribes, I could not give any official information to Congress, as I had anticipated, before going.

But, however, I hope the administration at present will not forget their verbal promise to me, through my friend the Hon. Abbott Lawrence—"That they will favor any humane measure which Congress, in its wisdom, may devise for the Indian Nations."

The only objection that I have to the country which I have named is the *nude state of the country* and the *lightness of its soil;* but this is not the only land which Congress might appropriate for such a purpose, as there are other lands which might be appropriated.

A scheme so vast and so important to the Indians, as well as to the relation of the general government with reference to the Indians, Congress, I hope, will take all the necessary consideration which its importance demands; and knowing we have your sympathy, I feel safe in the thought, that you will do justice to the Indian.

I herewith submit letters from the Governors of different States, and others, Mayors, and public men, in recommendation of my scheme; you will observe the kind tone of these letters as a true indication of the manner in which I have been kindly received all over the Union, in pursuance of this object.

My friends have, in some instances, been mistaken in the idea that I was seeking something else than to be placed in a position to do good; and though glad to think that they have been kind in their well wishes, the greatest kindness they will do me is, to aid me in my endeavors to do good to my unfortunate brethren in this country.

I have been desired to go over to the old world, and advocate the cause of my brethren in this country, by my friends. I choose not to do so until I have tried every laudable effort in this country. And if in presenting the subject, I have not presented it in the right spirit, pardon me; yea, at the same time I would invoke your forgiveness for past offenses for my brethren, and hope the accumulated responsibility which our forefathers, on both sides, have thrown upon us, will teach us both to do now, in this our day, what ought to have been done long ago.

In presenting this object before different legislative bodies, during the past season, they, as you are well aware, have passed resolutions, recommending the matter, and should it be necessary others will do so; but it does not seem, in my mind, that it is necessary, since the kindness which the Members of Congress have ever manifested. I shall place the whole of this matter for your disposal, and shall be anxious to see the result. During this winter, until spring, I hope to be in Washington.

LETTERS.

[*From* Chas. F. Manly, *and others.*]

Raleigh, N. C., March 22, 1849.

Hon. Thomas Ewing, Secretary of Home Department:

Sir—We understand that the Chippeway Chief, G. Copway, who visited this place during the late winter, and who has been lecturing in several States on the subject of confederating the Indian tribes with a view to their improvement and civilization, intends visiting the various tribes on our frontiers for the purpose of preparing them for the proposed scheme, and also examining that portion of our western territory where he proposes to locate them. We further learn that said Chief Copway wishes to obtain the protection of the general government as far as practicable, and that he may be accredited to the several Indian agencies on our frontiers, so as to obtain all the aid and information they may be able to afford him. You will please allow us to recommend said Copway to the protection of the general government, and to request, that if not considered incompatible with the functions of your department, he may be furnished with such credentials as will secure for him the assistance and protection of our Indian agents and other authorities of the government. Most respectfully,

Chas. F. Manly,
Wm. F. Collins,
W. Hill,
C. L. Hunton.

[*From* K. Rayner.]

Raleigh, N. C., March 21, 1849.

My Dear Sir—I received your very welcome letter to-day; and I assure you it was with pleasure I heard of the flattering reception you have met with in your travels, and the cheering prospects which may await your favorite and philanthropic project of concentrating and confederating the Indian tribes, with a view to their Christian improvement and education. You have my sincere and heart-felt wishes for your success. My own opinion is, that your labors have already to a great extent awakened the public mind to the importance of your great measure, and that you have only to persevere in order to command success.

The resolution in regard to this measure passed our Legislature at a late period of the session. We thought it best to wait till the press of business was somewhat through with; and I think it passed both Houses unanimously. Your request in regard to an application to the Home Department in your behalf for *credentials* which will enable you to visit the various Indian tribes on our frontiers, shall be attended to. I will endeavor to procure them in time to be forwarded in this letter. If I do not, I will forward them in a day or two.

I am much pleased with your design of visiting the various Indian tribes. Having in a great measure prepared the public mind for it among the "*pale faces*," you have now but to prepare the "*red men*" for it. I think a movement among the Indian tribes in favor of it, must secure its adoption.

The scheme in which you are engaged is a vast, a gigantic one. It is one which suggests to the philanthropic mind the most grand and lofty conceptions. Go on, and may Heaven prosper you. If you succeed, your name will go down to posterity identified with one of the most glorious movements of the age in which we live. If you fail now, you will, perhaps, have laid the foundation on which this mighty fabric, to be dedicated to Christian philanthropy, may be reared hereafter, under auspices more favorable than the present. At all events you will, when you come to die, have the ennobling reflection to console you, that you have devoted your life to the welfare of your race, and in endeavoring to prepare them for a paradise hereafter, immeasurably exceeding in happiness and glory that of the delightful "hunting grounds" promised them in the vague legends of their fathers.

I shall, I assure you, be happy at any and at all times to hear from you, especially of your adventures in the far-distant West.

Yours respectfully and sincerely,

K. RAYNER.

Rev. GEO. COPWAY, Boston, Mass.

[*Copy of a Letter from* GOV. BRIGGS, *of Mass., to Secretary of Home Department.*]

BOSTON, April 5, 1849.

DEAR SIR—During the past winter I have seen a good deal of the Rev. GEO. COPWAY, a Chippeway Chief, who is laboring to improve the condition of his brethren in the western country. I sympathize deeply with him in his philanthropic object, and wish him all possible success in his efforts to do good to the wasting and ill-fated remnant of his race.

By his lectures and demeanor while here, Mr. COPWAY has won the esteem and respect of many of the most respectable citizens of Boston, and created an interest in his humane and noble purpose.

I trust you will not deem it officious in me to express the hope that you will, so far as your judgment may approve, extend to him any aid in your power toward the promotion of his plan.

Respectfully and truly yours,
GEO. N. BRIGGS.

HON. THOS. EWING, Secretary of the Home Department.

I fully concur in the above.

EDWARD EVERETT.

CITY HALL, BOSTON, April 27, 1849.

I entirely concur in the preceding recommendation signed by Gov. Briggs and Gov. Everett. Mr. COPWAY has secured the respect and good will of the people of this vicinity generally, who feel a lively interest in the subject of his philanthropic labors, and who hope that his application to the government will receive favorable and effectual consideration.

JOHN P. BIGELOW.

[*Copy of Letter from* AMOS LAWRENCE, *of Boston, to Secretary of Home Department.*]

BOSTON, April 9, 1849.

At the request of GEORGE COPWAY, a Chippeway Chief, I beg leave to say that, during his visits here in the last two months, he has awakened a strong interest in many to have our national government consider how the race of "red men" can best be served to save them from wasting away, and how to elevate and educate them to enjoy the blessings of our common Father, no less than ourselves who occupy their lands. My friend Gov. Briggs, has given COPWAY a letter to you, sir, which I cordially subscribe to, and pray you to do what you can for this interesting and enterprising young Christian Indian, and preacher, and chief, and thus give a practical illustration of the strong foundation we have this way for our respect and confidence in your powers and your principles.

AMOS LAWRENCE.

To Hon. THOS. EWING,
Secretary of Home Department, Washington.

[*From* J. PRESCOTT HALL.]

NEW YORK, May 2, 1849.

DEAR SIR—This letter will be handed to you by the Rev. GEORGE COPWAY, the celebrated Indian Chief, KAH-GE-GA-GAH-BOUH of the Chippeway race.

This gentleman has been introduced to me by highly respectable persons of Boston, where Mr. COPWAY has resided some time, and made known his project of visiting the western Indian tribes, and his plans for their moral and religious improvement. I cannot doubt that Mr. COPWAY is a worthy person, and being requested by him, I beg leave to present him to your favorable notice.

With the highest respect,
Your obedient servant,
J. PRESCOTT HALL.

Hon. THOS. EWING, Secretary of Interior.

[*From* B. F. BUTLER.]

NEW YORK, May 7, 1849.

DEAR SIR—In common with other friends of the preservation and improvement of the aboriginal races of this continent, I beg leave to commend to your favorable consideration the suggestion which, as I understand, has been submitted to your consideration, of employing Mr. GEORGE COPWAY, a Chief of the Chippeway Nation, to collect information and otherwise aid in measures for the benefit of his people. To one who has so long enjoyed peculiar facilities like yourself for becoming acquainted with the history, condition and interests of the Indian tribes, it is superfluous that I should enter into any argument on the subject, for I doubt not your impressions as to the desirableness of promoting the permanent happiness of these tribes, and the high obligation resting on the government of the United States to engage in this work, are, to say the least, quite as decided, as I am sure they are quite as sincere and earnest as my own.

The object of my present note is, therefore, merely to enrol myself among those who take an interest in the labors to which Mr. COPWAY is devoted, and who desire to see him employed therein with the countenance and aid of the general government.

I am, sir, with high respect, your obedient servant,
B. F. BUTLER.

The Hon. THOS. EWING, Secretary of the Interior, Washington.

[*From* A. WHITNEY.]

NEW YORK, May 3, 1849.

SIR—I had the pleasure of meeting with the Rev. Mr. COPWAY, a Chippeway Chief, at different places where he has lectured, and have seen him at Washington during the past winter, and he has not only interested me deeply in the philanthropic enterprise to which his whole soul seems devoted, but also in himself as a man of intelligence and character.

He proposes visiting the north-western tribes of Indians during the coming summer, and if compatible with your views and duties, I feel that it would promote the cause of humanity to render him aid and protection.

I have myself visited several tribes of western savage Indians. Their old chiefs many of them are wise men, considering the light that has been revealed to them. They look forward to a time, when the game, their support, must disappear before civilization, and unless some new system can be introduced to change from their present life, they see no alternative but that they must soon disappear before the white man and their race become extinct. They are ready to commence a reform, but how is it to be brought about? Who is to accomplish it? May we hope that Providence is raising up Mr. Copway for that purpose?

With highest considerations, &c., &c., your obedient servant,

A. Whitney.

Hon. Thos. Ewing, Secretary Home Department.

[*From* W. F. Havemeyer.]

Mayor's Office, New York, May 5, 1849.

The Hon. Thomas Ewing, *Secretary of the Home Department:*

Mr. Geo. Copway, the Chippeway Chief, who has been lecturing here during the past season, on the subject of confederating the Indian tribes with a view to their improvement and civilization, desires, as I understand, visiting the various Indian tribes on our frontier, for the purpose of examining that portion of our western territory on which he proposes to locate them.

He desires to obtain the protection of the general government, and to be accredited to the several Indian agencies on our frontier, and I very cheerfully recommend him and his purpose as eminently entitled to the favor of every philanthropist, and if compatible with the arrangements of your department, such credentials as he desires would, I know, greatly facilitate his plans and will be worthily bestowed.

I have the honor to be, very respectfully, your obedient servant,

W. F. Havemeyer.

[*From* E. G. W. Squier.]

New York, May 10, 1849.

My Dear Sir—Allow me most earnestly to commend to your favorable consideration the objects which my friend Mr. George Copway, Chief of the Ojibwas Nation, has in view, and in behalf of which he will solicit the aid of the government. I have known Mr. Copway for a long time, and after much reflection, have no hesitation in saying that his designs are humane, generous and Christian, and that his plans are practicable and ought to be facilitated by all proper means, both by individuals and the government. The red race of Americans have my warm sympathies as I know they must have yours; and I feel assured that you will listen to Mr. Copway's plans, and take such means as you with propriety can to further them, in case they meet your enlightened approbation.

With my warmest regards, I am, sir, your obedient servant,

E. G. W. Squier.

Hon. Thos. Ewing, Secretary of the Interior.

[*From* PROFESSOR SILLIMAN.]

YALE COLLEGE, NEW HAVEN, November 22, 1849.

To the Rev. GEORGE COPWAY:

DEAR SIR—I have perused, with great interest and satisfaction the documents which you have been so kind as to place in my hands, in relation to your plan for the preservation and improvement of the Indian Nations. With many of the authors of those letters I am personally acquainted, and I am happy to say that I cordially concur with them in the views which they have communicated.

I have also listened, with much pleasure, to your lectures recently delivered here, and to your interesting and instructive remarks in personal interviews; and the effect on my own mind is, that of decided conviction that your plan is the best—perhaps the only plan that can save the remnants of the aboriginal nations of this Continent from extinction. I should have no confidence in its success were it not devised in the spirit of Christian benevolence, and brought forward by a Christian Chief, whose piety insures for him the confidence of the wise and the good—whose high intelligence must everywhere command respect, and whose conduct and manners as a gentleman conciliate the kindness of all those who have the pleasure of his acquaintance.

Being in no way connected with political plans, and being known to only one member of the Cabinet at Washington, it may not be in my power to serve you and your noble cause by any direct application in your behalf; but if this communication can be of any use, you are at liberty to dispose of it in any way that you may think proper.

With sentiments of high respect and esteem, and the best wishes for your success,

I remain, Rev. and Dear Sir,
Your friend, and the friend of the Red man,
B. SILLIMAN.

[*From* ALEXANDER RAMSEY.]

SAINT PAUL, MINNESOTA TER., September 9, 1849.

Hon. THOMAS EWING, Secretary Interior Department:

SIR—It was my pleasure, while I resided in the East, frequently to hear the Rev. Mr. COPWAY, a Chippeway Chief, address large audiences there, upon the subject of Christianizing and civilizing the various tribes of his race in North America, and the plan which he urged of concentrating them upon a comparatively confined portion of the country, and thus compelling them to abandon the chase for agriculture, struck me as promising much success.

He has recently been spending some time with us in Minnesota, and his views, I am pleased to know, are concurred in by the people here, who, from their long familiarity with the Indian races, know much of their character.

Other schemes for their amelioration have produced, I am sorry to say it, but few fruits; therefore, I trust an opportunity may be furnished of fully testing the project of Mr. Copway, by which the poor Indian, under the Providence of God, may yet be saved from total extinction.

I am not prepared to say that the region of country between the James river and the Missouri is that best adapted to the experiment. I fear the soil is too light, and the country too nude of timber, for a fine farming country. The Government, doubtless, in their extensive domain, have better land than this, which they would dedicate to such a purpose.

Very respectfully, your obedient servant,

Alex. Ramsey.

www.ingramcontent.com/pod-product-compliance
Lightning Source LLC
LaVergne TN
LVHW011132110826
845150LV00008B/2310
* 9 7 8 1 4 1 8 1 9 4 0 5 5 *